CRAPPY

to

Happy

LOVE WHO
YOU'RE WITH

CRAPPY

to

Happy

LOVE WHO
YOU'RE WITH

CASSANDRA DUNN

Hardie Grant

BOOKS

Cassandra Dunn is a clinical and coaching psychologist and an experienced mindfulness educator, workshop facilitator and keynote speaker. Cass is the expert psychologist for trainer Tiffiny Hall's online health and fitness program, tiffxo.com, and she regularly shares her insights on happiness, mindfulness and wellbeing in print and digital media. She also hosts the wildly popular *Crappy to Happy* podcast, which has had millions of downloads. Cass lives on the Sunshine Coast in Queensland with her husband, daughter and a menagerie of rescued animals. This is her third book.

Connect with Cass online

facebook: **facebook.com/cassdunn.xo**

instagram/twitter: **cassdunn_xo**

cassdunn.com

To my parents, Greg & Kathy Lyons,
for being positive relationship role models
for over 40 years.

CONTENTS

———

CONTENTS

___

INTRODUCTION

> Whether you consider yourself to be a loner or a people person, an extrovert or an introvert, we all have a fundamental need for human connection.

This isn't a 'nice to have'. Research clearly demonstrates that positive relationships are essential for our physical and mental wellbeing. And yet, despite the explosion of new technologies that allow us to communicate with anyone, anywhere, at any time, we're lonelier than we've ever been.

Some might even argue that it's that very same technology that is causing us to feel so isolated. We all know what it's like to compete with someone's phone for their attention, and, if we're honest, most of us are just as guilty of being distracted by our own devices. Despite the threat that technology can pose to intimacy and rapport, the option of online communication as a supplement to face-to-face interaction has been shown to actually *reduce* feelings of loneliness. So, it seems we can't blame small screens entirely for our troubles, but we could probably be a little more mindful about how we engage with them.

It seems more likely to me that in our endlessly busy lives, we're so focused on the pursuit of our own goals that we're failing to intentionally carve out time for the people who matter most. With the high value our society places on individual success and achievement, we're conditioned to keep moving, doing, achieving and acquiring, whereas the depth of connection necessary for our wellbeing requires us to slow down and sit still. When do we have the time?

We're also highly mobile, with abundant opportunities to follow our chosen path no matter where it might lead us, whether to a faraway city or even across the globe. But every time we pack up our lives and move to a new location, we leave behind whatever local connections we'd established, and have to start again somewhere else. The older we get, the harder it is to forge the kind of deep, trusting relationships that are often built over a long, shared history. The fuller our lives are with personal obligations and responsibilities, the less available time we have to put the required effort into establishing and maintaining new relationships.

And what about the role of individual differences? We each have our own complex mix of personality and personal history. Most of us are never taught that our early interactions create blueprints for our subsequent relationships, so we're left feeling puzzled and frustrated by our own self-defeating relationship patterns – or worse, we blame others for our inability to cultivate authentic, meaningful relationships.

Social conventions often dictate that we focus on fitting in and keeping the peace, even if that means compromising our own values or staying quiet about how we really feel. We're taught as children to share and say sorry, but many of us weren't taught the importance of knowing, valuing and trusting ourselves, so that we don't need someone else's approval. How do we hope to build genuine, authentic connections on a foundation of approval-seeking and people-pleasing?

In my first book, *Crappy to Happy: Simple Steps to Live Your Best Life*, I devoted a chapter to the importance of social connections because of the significant role that relationships play in the overall quality of our life. In the time since that book was published, I've reflected a lot on the quality of connections in my own life and the things that get in the way of consistent, positive connection.

I often blame a lack of time for the extended gaps in contact with my friends or family. And I know enough to realise that whenever the excuse is time, what we're really talking about are priorities. We all choose how we spend our time. If we don't truly value and appreciate the people in our social networks, it's very easy to relegate them to the bottom of a long list of more pressing responsibilities. How we choose to spend our time is often a reflection of our values. If the way you're spending your time is not a reflection of what's truly most important to you, that might be a timely wake-up call to start being more intentional in how you invest your time. After all, it's your most important resource.

Interestingly, in the months since I began writing this book, the world has been affected by the spread of the novel coronavirus, for which there is currently no treatment or cure. Our only protection against a disease that is killing hundreds of thousands of people, forcing us to close our borders domestically and internationally, is for people to stay away from each other. The terms 'social distancing' and 'self-isolation' have become a part of our shared vernacular, *globally*.

Suddenly, the way for us to best look after ourselves and each other is to have no physical contact with

"How we choose to spend our time is often a reflection of our values."

the people we hold dear. Children can't hug their grandparents or play sport with their friends. Work colleagues can't gather around the water cooler and talk about their weekends. Given how essential our relationships are to our physical and mental health, it's difficult to know what the long-term effects of this forced separation will be, but what we've witnessed is the emergence of new and creative ways of staying connected. We've also become acutely aware of those who are most alone and therefore the most vulnerable in our communities, including the elderly and disabled.

If there is an upside (and there will surely be many) to this crisis, it might be that it's given us a chance to slow down and spend quality time with those in our immediate family, and that when it's over, we will appreciate more than ever the value of our social networks.

Perhaps we'll have come to see which relationships are truly of value in our lives and need to be nurtured with our time and attention. The opportunity for time alone might have given us the opportunity to reflect on our values and realign our priorities, forging connections that are intentional rather than habitual.

By the time you're holding this book in your hand, it's my greatest hope that you're savouring the joy of sitting side by side with your loved ones, sharing a meal with friends, feeling the warmth of a hug or the assurance of a handshake or an arm around your shoulder. I hope you're revelling in the camaraderie of attending a sports match, the joy of live music, or just sharing space with people who have discovered the real value of human connection.

Step one

PUT PEOPLE FIRST

> Life's most joyful moments and its most painful ones often arise out of our interactions with others.

If you've been fortunate enough to have people in your life who love and support you, and who are genuinely invested in your happiness and wellbeing, you will know what a tremendous source of comfort, strength and joy that is. And equally, if you've opened your heart to someone, you may have felt the heartbreak of loss or the sadness of a fractured relationship with a friend.

Our relationships are central to our happiness; and yet, we're not giving them anywhere near the time or attention they deserve. When we're surrounded by a supportive social circle and enjoying all the benefits that come from quality connections, we give little thought to just how important those relationships are, or what our life might be like without them. In other words, we take people for granted. In fact, it's often only when circumstances change, and for whatever reason we find ourselves without access to an available network of close companions, that we begin to realise just how precious it is to have someone we can truly count on. The fact is, loneliness is an epidemic, and one that's on the rise.

Meanwhile, we're all keeping busy leading full, productive lives, striving to achieve meaningful goals. We're climbing career ladders, chasing entrepreneurial dreams, raising children and exploring the world – ostensibly in the pursuit of happiness. But how often do we intentionally set goals to increase our social engagement or to improve the quality of our connections? If we had a more complete understanding of just how profoundly our health, happiness and even our mortality is impacted by the quality of our social interactions, perhaps we might pause to reassess our priorities.

SOCIAL CONNECTION AND MENTAL HEALTH

We now have reams of research to prove what we've instinctively always known. Not only do you feel more positive when you have positive people around you, you're also far less likely to suffer from depression, anxiety or other mood disorders when you have satisfying connections.

These connections mean you're also likely to have higher self-esteem, greater empathy and be more trusting and cooperative, which in turn makes others more willing to trust and cooperate with you. Satisfying social connections therefore create a lovely, positive, self-reinforcing loop.

You might be wondering what comes first – is it that having strong social connections boosts your mood and buffers you against depression, or do happier people just naturally attract more friends? Researchers in New Zealand performed a fairly comprehensive study to explore this, and concluded that while the relationship definitely goes both ways, social connectedness predicted subsequent mental health far more strongly than mental health predicted subsequent social connectedness.

We also now know, thanks to a large survey conducted in Germany, that when people set goals related to increasing or improving social engagement (e.g. 'I plan to spend more time with family and friends') they report greater life satisfaction a year later, compared to those who pursue more self-focused, non-social goals (e.g. 'I plan to find a better job'). Clearly, there are rewards to be gained from being proactive and intentional in your effort to improve your social life.

Perhaps the most compelling argument for focusing attention on social connectedness has come from the Harvard Study of Adult Development (the Grant study), which began in 1938 with a cohort of 268 male Harvard graduates. The study has tracked every aspect of the men's lives for over 80 years with a view to identify the psychosocial determinants of healthy ageing. A separate cohort of 456 disadvantaged, inner-city youth was later added to the study. Robert Waldinger, who has directed the study since 2005, has famously reported that after taking into account every factor in the men's lives, including things like their job and income, health habits, alcohol use, community involvement and marital satisfaction, the single biggest predictor of happiness into their old age was the quality of their social connections.

Those connections, whether they be with close, supportive friends, a happy marriage or active involvement in the community, didn't only make them happier, they also had a startling positive effect on their physical wellbeing. This just reinforces what we've learned in the past three decades about the undeniable physical health benefits that arise from having strong social and emotional support.

SOCIAL CONNECTEDNESS AND PHYSICAL HEALTH

People who are socially isolated or lonely get sick more often, take longer to recover and are more likely to relapse than those who have satisfying social connections.

While 'social isolation' refers to the experience of having a limited number of social connections and is therefore objective and quantifiable, 'loneliness' refers to the subjective experience of how *satisfied* a person is with their relationships. Most of us know from experience that it's possible to be completely alone but feel very emotionally connected; equally, you can be in a crowded room or in a marriage and feel deeply lonely. While those two experiences are subjectively different, researchers don't identify any real difference when it comes to the negative impact they have on your health and wellbeing.

Julianne Holt-Lunstad is a Belgian psychologist and researcher who collated hundreds of studies conducted over several years, examining the links between social connectedness and physical health. Her groundbreaking findings highlighted that the quality of our connections is as significant a predictor of early mortality (if not more so) as other well-established health risks, such as smoking, excessive alcohol use, obesity and untreated hypertension. Isolation increases the risk of heart disease by 29 per cent and stroke by 32 per cent. The risk of early death increases by around 40 per cent for people who report a lack of meaningful social connections.

The health risks of social isolation and loneliness aren't limited to any one particular age group. One review compared people's level of social integration with physical indicators of poor health across the lifespan. In adolescents, inflammation in the body was more strongly associated with social isolation than with lack of physical activity. In old age, being isolated posed a higher risk for developing diabetes than having hypertension. Perhaps when medical professionals are assessing our risk of disease and death, they should enquire about the quality of our social connections as well as our weight, cholesterol level and blood pressure.

While none of us, regardless of age, genetics or lifestyle, is immune to the health risks of poor social connections, it's older people who are of most concern. They are already likely to be experiencing declining health, and their isolation increases as friends and loved ones die, children and grandchildren move away and their choice to remain independent may mean they live alone with limited social contact. As their health and mobility deteriorates, outings become more difficult. On a practical level, there might not be anyone to check that there's enough food in the fridge or that prescriptions are filled, or to help them to get to appointments. On a personal level, they're starving for human contact.

Loneliness in older people is associated with significantly increased risk of aged care home admissions, higher blood pressure, and a 40 per cent higher risk of dementia. One study of 1600 older adults found that almost half of them reported feeling lonely, and of those who were lonely, 23 per cent died within six years, compared with only 14 per cent of those who didn't feel lonely. The lonely older people also experienced greater declines in their physical and mental health, including decreased mobility. This is another one of those feedback loops, but this time a vicious cycle of reduced health leading to more isolation.

Even if you think you can live perfectly well without human company, too much solitude may eventually take a heavy toll on your health and happiness.

WHY IS LONELINESS SO LETHAL?

To understand why social disconnection is so disastrous to our health we need to do a quick review of how we evolved as a species. When our ancestors walked the earth as hunter-gatherers, whether they belonged to a group or were left alone was quite literally a matter of life and death. A lone cave person couldn't fend off a hungry predator or hostile enemy, whereas in unity, there was protection and strength. One person could stand guard while someone else slept. Early forms of communication, cooperation and the sharing of resources led to the development of more sophisticated tools and technology, which increased the likelihood of survival and reproduction. Food was shared so no-one went hungry, and children were raised under the watchful eye of the whole village. Social connectedness was necessary for survival.

Being cut off from the group would trigger your primitive brain's alarm system, alerting you to danger. The activation of our instinctive threat response causes a flood of stress hormones such as adrenaline and cortisol to be released into the bloodstream. Even after thousands of years of biological evolution, the tiny almond-shaped part of the brain known as the amygdala is still very effectively doing its job of alerting us to potential threats and mobilising our fight or flight response. And after thousands of years, it still considers social isolation and loneliness to be threats to your safety.

Our biologically driven need for social belonging and acceptance is still paramount.

MODERN-DAY THREATS

These days, we're not typically in danger of being speared by an enemy or mauled by a bear. We usually have enough to eat and a roof over our heads. With those basic needs being met and the deadliest threats not on our radar, our amygdala, still keen to protect us, tends to be on the lookout for signs that we're being excluded from social networks, being judged by our peers, upsetting a friend, making a social faux pas or not fitting in. The most common phobia experienced by people is the fear of public speaking (more common than the fear of heights, spiders or even death itself), which shows just how important it is for us to avoid negative social appraisal or rejection.

If loneliness is the feeling of dissatisfaction that arises from poor-quality social connections – that is, it's the sense that you don't have access to a supportive social network – you can be absolutely sure it's going to set off your inner alarm.

The threat response is designed to be short and sharp, priming your body to run from danger or go into battle. When the stressful situation is prolonged, the continual drip-feed of stress hormones into your bloodstream creates a toxic load on your nervous system. Over time, this creates inflammation in your body, compromising your health and interfering with many important physiological processes, including those of your immune, digestive and reproductive systems. It elevates your blood pressure and puts pressure on your heart. Sleep quality is compromised, creating a cascade of negative consequences for your physical and mental health.

The links between the quality of your social relationships and your physical wellbeing suddenly become very clear. Is it any wonder that feeling lonely or lacking meaningful social connections has such devastating consequences for our physical and mental health?

PRIORITISE RELATIONSHIPS

Create community

You don't need a lot of people in your life but you do need a high-quality few. To strengthen or expand your social network, look to groups you're already connected with and find opportunities to strengthen a sense of community. School, work, neighbours, local interest groups or charities are all good places to start building a network.

Phone a friend

If you have existing friendships that have been neglected, make the effort to connect. Pick up the phone or arrange to meet for coffee or lunch. Quality friendships wither without regular injections of time, effort and energy.

Set a meaningful goal to increase social engagement

When you're looking ahead and setting goals you'd like to achieve in the coming months, remember that social engagement goals are the most likely to bring you lasting fulfilment (and maybe even boost your health and add years to your life). Add a social goal to your list.

Step two

UNDERSTAND ATTACHMENT

From the moment you were born, the way your parents engaged with you laid the foundations for the way you'd participate in subsequent relationships.

Even before you developed language skills, your brain began constructing an internal working model of how relationships work, much like a template or a blueprint. The very fact that those blueprints are created pre-verbally means they're stored outside your conscious awareness. They're like the software running in the background of your computer. You don't necessarily see it or know how it works, but it contains a lot of 'If, then' type algorithms, which dictate what's most likely to happen in any given scenario.

John was a client of mine who was warm and good-natured, with a wide range of interests. He grew up in a stable family home, got a great education and has a successful career. He makes friends easily and is happily married. Occasionally though, people close to John notice that he retreats socially, stops returning calls and doesn't engage in the usual cheery banter at work. John told me that when something is bothering him – if he's frustrated at work or his golf game is off, for example – he becomes almost impossible to live with. He knows he'd feel better if he just talked about how he feels, but he says it's like being trapped behind a wall. He can see the people he cares about on the other side but is completely unable to reach them.

Another client, Leila, told me there was a lot of conflict in her family home when she was growing up, which meant she moved out and became independent very early. She married her childhood sweetheart, but over time the relationship became difficult. Her husband became increasingly verbally abusive, so Leila ended the marriage. She's recently commenced a new relationship

"The root cause of these kinds of problems can often be found by digging into your earliest attachment experiences."

with a stable, loving partner who treats her well. But no matter how healthy the relationship is, Leila feels like she's always waiting for the other shoe to drop. She's jealous and insecure, looking for problems where none exist. She constantly seeks reassurance from her partner, but no matter how much she hears that she's safe and loved, the message doesn't stick. She can't seem to develop any sense of emotional safety at all.

Both John and Leila are frustrated with themselves, but feel powerless to change the behaviours that they know are driving a wedge in their relationships. The root cause of these kinds of problems can often be found by digging into your earliest attachment experiences.

ENTER 'ATTACHMENT THEORY'

British psychologist John Bowlby first proposed a theory of attachment in the 1950s to describe the instinctive process infants use to bond with their caregivers. He described attachment as 'a lasting psychological connectedness between human beings'. As an evolutionary process, it's bred into the biology of human infants and their caregivers as a way of ensuring our survival.

This attachment relationship comprises a series of interactions, cues and responses exchanged back and forth between the infant and their main carer. When a child has a sense that their parent or carer is physically and psychologically present, they feel safe to explore their environment. The parent becomes a secure base from which the baby can go out, play and engage with the world. When they've had enough exploring and want to come back to share their joy, to feel safe or to just get a cuddle, the parent creates a safe haven for their return.

At the most basic level, the child signals a need through a noise, gesture or facial expression. When mum or dad responds appropriately to meet that need (and when this happens on a consistent basis), a secure attachment is formed. Perhaps the most important part of the relationship is that the parent needs to be physically and emotionally available to attend to those subtle signals and respond in a timely, sensitive and appropriate manner.

If the baby sends out the signal and for whatever reason, mum or dad isn't able to respond, there's a problem in the system. Human babies are so highly attuned to their caregiver that they'll quickly adapt their own behaviour. First, they may try harder to get through to their loved one. Later, if all their attempts fail, they may actually protect themselves from further emotional harm by shutting down their attachment system. What you learn in those early interactions, you carry through life.

In the 1970s another psychologist, Mary Ainsworth, identified very distinct attachment patterns based on the nature of those interactions between the child and parent. This is where it gets interesting. She discovered that by around 12–18 months of age, children will very accurately demonstrate their inner working model of relationships through their behaviour. If the system is working as it should, children will develop a secure attachment. But in roughly 40 per cent of cases, they develop an insecure attachment.

It's important to understand that your attachment needs don't change across your lifespan. We all have the same instinctive drive to form bonds, to be seen, heard, felt and understood. We all want to be able to turn to someone for comfort when we're distressed, to be appreciated, enjoyed and valued for who we are. Your attachment system is always attuned to whether your

"Your attachment needs don't change across your lifespan."

needs for proximity and comfort are being met, at first by your parents and later by friends and romantic partners.

The attachment style you developed as a child forms the groundwork of how you relate to others. If the attachment style was insecure and endures into adulthood, the strategies you adopted to cope with an unavailable or inconsistent caregiver might start playing out in your adult relationships and we may start to see the kinds of problems John and Leila experienced.

LET'S TALK ABOUT ATTACHMENT STYLES

Typically, attachment styles are described as four discrete categories. The first is 'autonomous' or secure, and each of the three insecure attachment patterns represents people's particular vulnerabilities or sensitivities. It's more helpful (and more accurate) to think of your attachment pattern as a representation of where you fall on just two dimensions: anxious and avoidant.

Anxious attachment involves being concerned about rejection or abandonment, whereas avoidant attachment is more to do with whether you feel comfortable relying on others or if you emotionally withdraw during times of need. An individual can score highly on one dimension or the other, or high or low on both. This is a helpful way to understand the four distinct attachment categories, but it's important to realise that no-one is always secure all of the time. We all have anxious and avoidant tendencies that are likely to show themselves during times of relationship stress.

Autonomous

If you were one of the fortunate individuals who had caregivers who offered you timely, sensitive, emotionally attuned caregiving on a consistent basis, you likely developed a secure attachment as a child (which we call 'autonomous' as an adult). Having a secure attachment pattern means you score low on both the anxious and avoidant scales. This makes you feel emotionally secure, comfortable with intimacy, confident you'll have your needs met, and willing to trust others. If you have an autonomous attachment style, you likely regulate your emotions more effectively, so you enjoy better mental health, increased empathy and higher self-esteem.

Of course, having a secure attachment style is an advantage, because it means being less emotionally reactive, less likely to take things too personally and means you will be comfortable with closeness but not threatened by distance. It's not the only factor determining how successful and fulfilling your adult relationships will be, but it offers a very solid foundation.

Preoccupied

If your parents were not consistent in their caregiving – for example, if they were sometimes calm and nurturing and at other times reacted with extreme anger – you might have developed an anxious attachment style because you never quite knew what to expect. If your parents were overly intrusive in your life or relied on you to meet their emotional needs, you'd also likely develop an anxious style of relating. In adulthood, this is referred to as 'preoccupied' and reflects high anxiety and low avoidance, making you highly sensitive to possible rejection by others and threatened by too much distance in a relationship. You might constantly seek reassurance to soothe your anxiety, but never feel completely at ease.

Adults with a preoccupied attachment don't fully trust that people will be consistently available. Your internal alarm system is activated by even the subtlest signs that someone might be upset with you or rejecting of you. You make constant bids for attention, needing to be reassured that someone loves you, always texting, calling or wanting to be close. It's understandable that someone whose parents were inconsistently available when they were a child often has a hard time trusting that people will be consistently available as an adult, but this anxious, insecure behaviour can ultimately drive people away.

Dismissive-avoidant

If your parents were physically absent due to death or divorce, or emotionally unavailable because of mental health issues, substance use or simply not being emotionally attuned and sensitive, you might have developed an avoidant attachment style. You picked up early on that it's risky to get too emotionally close and connected to someone, and so you respond by pretending you don't have emotional needs. You stop seeking comfort or connection and adopt the view that you're on your own to deal with challenges in life. As an adult, this is referred to as 'dismissive-avoidant' and refers to the combination of high avoidance and low anxiety. As a result, your inner alarm system is activated by too much intimacy and your response is to shut down emotionally and withdraw. You're the person who enjoys a lot of personal space and is fine without a lot of emotional intimacy. It doesn't feel natural or comfortable to share too much vulnerability. You're the kind of person who doesn't often ask for help because you've internalised the message that people aren't willing to be there for you. When relationships get too close, maybe you lose interest. This is your way of keeping yourself safe. Interestingly, as soon as there is distance, those loving feelings return because the threat of intimacy has been removed, so if you have a dismissive-avoidant attachment style, pay attention to how you feel about the person when they're not around.

Fearful-avoidant

A fourth category was added to describe those children who didn't appear to have a coherent attachment pattern at all. These children displayed odd and inconsistent behaviours as a result of abusive or neglectful caregiving relationships. When a parent or caregiver is simultaneously the source of the child's distress and also the person they would normally turn to for comfort, they are placed in an impossible situation, and this creates damaging emotional, psychological and even physical consequences. Only around 5 per cent of the population is thought to have a disorganised attachment style.

In adulthood, this is called 'fearful-avoidant' and describes someone who scores high on both the anxious and avoidant dimensions, simultaneously wanting and fearing closeness. People with this pattern often have a negative view of themselves and look to others for approval, but can also have a deep distrust of others, always fearful of rejection or betrayal. People with a fearful-avoidant attachment tend to be highly dependent on others but also emotionally reserved and guarded.

EARNED SECURITY

It's easy to see how attachment patterns can affect your willingness to be vulnerable and trust others, to offer emotional support to others or to ask for help when you need it. The good news is that while your early attachment experiences will influence your thoughts, feelings and behaviours in subsequent relationships, your 'internal working model' continues to be updated and revised in light of your later relationship experiences. This means it is absolutely possible for your attachment orientation to change. This usually comes about through self-reflection, by making sense of your own early experiences and also by having healthy adult relationships that provide corrective emotional experiences.

The first step towards any change is to recognise the problem, and this means looking honestly at yourself, the kinds of relationships you're drawn to and how you typically deal with difficult emotions. What kinds of behaviours that you've spent a lifetime justifying are really manifestations of early attachment difficulties?

DEVELOPING SECURE ATTACHMENT

Practise mindfulness

Mindfulness meditation is the practice of turning towards your thoughts and feelings with an attitude of acceptance, curiosity and kindness. When you're able to notice your thoughts and feelings in the moment that they're occurring, tune in and get curious about them, rather than reacting in old, knee-jerk ways, you begin the process of healing and learning to choose a new response.

Choose wisely

Some people just aren't good for you and that's not anyone's fault. If you realise you have an anxious attachment and need a lot of emotional closeness, pairing up with someone who is avoidant is only going to reactivate old wounds and perpetuate an unhealthy cycle. You can both work on moving towards a secure attachment, but it's important to realise that it might be difficult to do that work while you're together.

Pause, then do something different

The path from insecurity to security takes more than just awareness. It requires you to choose a different action: to move away from what you've always done. If you're compelled to ask for reassurance, pause. Practise self-soothing instead. If you're inclined to shut down and withdraw, pause. Connect with someone instead. And if you have a secure attachment and you're inclined to be frustrated and impatient with someone else's behaviour, pause. Be compassionate.

Step three

LOOK FOR
PATTERNS

Spending time reflecting on your family of origin and deepening your understanding of attachment styles can provide tremendous insight into the patterns you see playing out in your relationships.

You might have spotted some of your own habitual patterns of thinking and reacting, and hopefully now you can see them as clever (if slightly ineffective) strategies designed to protect you from emotional harm or to ensure your needs are met.

You might also have noticed you have a tendency to choose the same kind of person over and over, or to continually recreate an unhealthy relationship dynamic, and you're at a loss to understand why. Attachment styles can fill in part of the story for you, but there's often more to it than that.

Schema theory was developed by psychologist Jeffrey Young in the 1980s. When something happens consistently in your life, your brain is very quick to create mental shortcuts to help you navigate life more efficiently. We've already established that your earliest relationships laid down blueprints for your future relationships in the form of attachment patterns.

In their self-help book *Reinventing Your Life*, Jeffrey Young and Janet Klosko also use the term 'lifetraps' to describe how these blueprints can get in the way of your ability to enjoy healthy, satisfying relationships. You may see the overlaps between attachment patterns and schemas, but schema theory digs more deeply into the specific behaviour patterns that people commonly develop as a result of early experiences. Those experiences may occur within your immediate family, or they might happen later in life – for example, if you're bullied at school or have another significant traumatic experience.

A 'schema' in psychology is a kind of mental framework that helps you make sense of life's experiences.

HOW SCHEMAS WORK

As children, we all have some basic emotional needs. When those needs aren't met, the only thing we can do is find a way to cope. Our developing brains are incredibly efficient at working out what the family dynamic is and adjusting our thoughts and responses to maintain a sense of psychological safety. Whatever situation you find yourself in, whether it's being harshly criticised or punished, compared unfavourably to your siblings, held to unrealistically high standards or having no limits set at all, you quickly establish that this is how things are. You know your place within that world, you understand what to expect from others and what's expected of you.

Schema theory can get complex and explaining it in detail is well beyond the scope of this book, but I do think it's helpful to have a broad understanding of the various 'lifetraps' that could be undermining your ability to enjoy healthy relationships. A schema is a mixture of your thoughts and feelings, memories and body sensations. Let's say you lost a parent early in life through death or divorce and you developed an *abandonment* schema. (You will know now that this could also create an insecure attachment.) The schema for abandonment includes an expectation that important people will leave you suddenly and you'll be left alone. It might involve early memories of being sad, helpless and confused, and sensations of tightness in your chest or a pit in your stomach.

Later, that schema might be activated every time a loved one walks out the door to go to work. Although the schema was formed in the past, it has a way of showing up in the present. You find yourself experiencing all those thoughts, feelings and sensations even though they have nothing to do with your current situation. If this is the case, the people in your life probably struggle to understand why you're reacting so intensely to an everyday situation, and you might also be unable to explain it.

THE COMFORT OF DISCOMFORT

What makes schemas so powerful and hard to shift is that we all find comfort in what we know. Even if your early experiences were painful, they are what's most familiar to you. You might not *like* feeling lonely or defective or unworthy of love, but if those feelings are familiar to you, you may gravitate towards situations that recreate them, because at least you know what to do in that situation. You might not like living with someone who is overly critical, judgemental or punitive, but if it's what you've grown up with, there is an ease in knowing what your role is in that situation.

Our brains love familiarity and predictability. They like it when they can doze off and conserve energy while we go about all our standard habits and routines. When you start changing things up and going off script, your brain has to wake up and start using energy to work out what this new thing is that you're trying to do. When that happens, and you start moving into new and unfamiliar territory (even if that territory is a safe, loving

"What makes schemas so powerful and hard to shift is that we all find comfort in what we know."

partnership where you're treated with respect and kindness), your brain only recognises that it's *different* and therefore potentially dangerous.

The same instinct for self-preservation that led you to create those schemas in the first place will start working to make sure you keep them intact. This is why changing those old habits takes a lot of patience, self-compassion and inner work. But it's work that's worth doing, and it all starts with recognising your own (or your friend's or partner's) predominant, unhelpful schemas.

COMMON UNHELPFUL SCHEMAS

Every child needs security, stability, affection, autonomy, healthy limits, self-expression and play if they're to grow into emotionally healthy, resilient adults. When those needs aren't met, the child develops a schema to help them cope. The schemas (or operating models) make perfect sense in the context of the unhealthy situation. It's when they're activated later on in normal, healthy scenarios that they create problems.

There are five categories of unhelpful schemas, and each of them relates to a specific set of emotional needs that haven't been met. Within each of those five domains, there are several distinct schemas that arise out of different experiences or family dynamics. You'll start to get a sense of how detailed and specific schemas can be, but also notice that there's a lot of potential for overlap.

Disconnection/rejection

When your basic needs for stability, security, love and nurturing aren't met in a consistent and predictable way in your early life, you may form an internal working model that has a central theme of disconnection or rejection.

One of those is the *abandonment* schema mentioned earlier. Another is the *emotional deprivation* schema, which is the expectation that you won't receive empathy, nurturing or emotional guidance. As you can imagine, this schema develops where there is a lack of warmth and emotional connection.

If you develop a *social exclusion* schema, you sense that you'll always be on the outer, feeling separate and isolated from groups or communities. It might be that your family belonged to a particular religious group that kept themselves separate, or you felt like a loner or were bullied at school.

A *defectiveness/shame* schema is the feeling that you're somehow flawed, inferior, bad, unwanted or unlovable. It might come from having harsh or critical parents, or from growing up in a house where there was a lot of secrecy and shame because of violence or substance abuse.

The *mistrust/abuse* schema is self-explanatory. If you've been abused or neglected as a child, you may have formed a core belief that you will always be mistreated.

Impaired autonomy and performance

If you grew up with overprotective parents or if your confidence was frequently undermined and you weren't given opportunities to develop autonomy and self-confidence, you may have formed a core belief that you're not capable of surviving on your own.

The schemas that might develop in this kind of environment include *dependence/incompetence*, which is the belief that you can't take care of yourself, make decisions or solve problems on your own, and have to rely on others.

The *failure* schema is the pervasive belief that you're bound to fail because you're inept, inferior or lacking talent. When there's a failure lifetrap at play, it's hard to form relationships on an equal footing.

You might choose partners who are successful as a way of boosting your own self-image, or you might try to compensate for your feelings of inferiority by focusing excessively on superficial qualities like appearance, and avoid the kind of depth that might reveal your own perceived flaws.

Impaired limits

Children need healthy limits and boundaries to feel safe and protected. When those limits aren't set and children are overindulged or spoiled, they can grow up with a schema of *entitlement/grandiosity*. You'd be right in assuming this can look a lot like narcissism. In some cases, it might manifest as demanding others take care of you, lacking empathy, and only associating with people you think are as special and deserving as you are.

Overvigilance/inhibition

If you grow up in a home where your childlike need for spontaneity and play is stifled by parents who are very strict or demanding, or who place a high value on achievement and good behaviour at the expense of fun and relaxation, you might develop an *unrelenting standards* schema. Typically, this can manifest as perfectionism, having very rigid rules, or being very critical of yourself and other people. You might also have difficulty expressing your emotions, be prone to negativity or pessimism, or be intolerant of or impatient with other people.

Other-directedness

When a child's healthy instinct to express their own needs is suppressed and instead the focus is on the needs of the parent or caregiver, they may grow up feeling that love is conditional on making their parents happy, and might develop a *subjugation* or *self-sacrificing* schema. I know a lot of women who've developed this pattern of feeling that they need to put their own needs last and cater instead to everyone else as a way of gaining love and approval. The constant focus on others instead of yourself can ultimately lead to anger and resentment, which obviously gets in the way of happy, balanced and mutually supportive relationships.

WHAT DO YOU DO WITH AN UNHEALTHY SCHEMA?

Much like attachment styles, schemas are typically running in the background, outside of your conscious awareness. You might recognise that you're a bit anxious or a perfectionist, or that you constantly defer to others, but you've been blaming yourself for this as if it's some kind of character flaw when really, it's a natural response to your earlier experience.

Remember that a schema is an internal experience. It's a bunch of thoughts and feelings, ideas and expectations, but your *behaviour* is not part of the schema. In fact, different people with the same schema might behave very differently – this is why schemas can be hard to spot!

The three typical behaviour strategies that people use when a schema is triggered are: counterattack (or overcompensate), escape/avoid or surrender. It helps to think of the three coping strategies as the 'fight, flight or freeze' responses in action.

Counterattack

When you go on the counterattack or try to overcompensate for your schema, you rebel against it, acting as if the opposite of the schema is true. It can be a very healthy and useful thing to challenge your schema, but with overcompensation, people tend to overshoot the mark and ultimately create more problems. For example, if you have a defectiveness schema, overcompensating might mean you behave as if you're superior to everyone around you as a way of masking your core feelings of inadequacy.

Escape/avoid

When escape or avoidance is your coping strategy, you set up your life in a certain way to avoid activating your schema. You might avoid relationships altogether, or you might avoid discussing anything too personal or vulnerable. Avoidance as a coping strategy is quite similar to the behaviours you see with an avoidant attachment style. Emotional avoidance can also involve doing things that block out or numb the painful thoughts and feelings associated with your schema, such as drinking, drugs, promiscuous sex, overeating, compulsively cleaning or being endlessly busy.

Surrender

When you surrender to a schema, you yield to it, accepting it as true. You don't bother trying to avoid it or fight it. Without even realising what you're doing, you continue to play out schema-driven patterns, recreating the childhood conditions that produced the schema in the first place. To use the abandonment example, surrendering to your schema would mean continually choosing partners who are emotionally unavailable, physically distant or unable to commit. Essentially, when you surrender, you accept your beliefs are true and stop expecting anything different, and therefore you create situations where your schema is continually reinforced.

BREAKING PATTERNS

Be honest with yourself

Awareness of a problem is always the first step to changing it, but it can be difficult to acknowledge the truth about your past experience or to tell the truth about what you think and feel. I hope that this overview has given you a good starting point for recognising how your experiences in your family or with your peers growing up have potentially created unhelpful beliefs and self-defeating patterns in your life.

Be kind and be patient

Longstanding, heavily entrenched patterns of
behaviour that have served a protective function in
your life don't change overnight. Learning to do things
differently will take time and require a lot of self-
compassion and patience. Similarly, if you recognise
any of these patterns in someone you love it's
important not to expect miracles.

Ask for help

Sometimes this work will require the assistance of trusted friends or even a trained therapist. Remember that if you have difficulty trusting a therapist, acknowledging you need help or expressing your truth, that in itself is likely to be due to your unhelpful schema. Challenging those thoughts and feelings is very much a part of your healing process.

Step four

KNOW
YOURSELF WELL

Before you can effectively build
a healthy, mutually rewarding
relationship, it's essential that you
truly know yourself and feel good
about who you are and what you
have to offer.

If you don't start with that foundation of self-awareness
and self-acceptance, you may look to someone else
to give you a sense of identity, or become consumed
with meeting someone else's needs because you're
disconnected from your own.

When you're not comfortable with who you are, you
may find yourself pretending to be something you're not

as a way of gaining others' approval or validation. If you doubt your own worthiness, you'll place undue emphasis on other people's opinions of you. If you're always looking to others to make you feel good about yourself, you're putting unfair pressure on those people, who want to be in a relationship with an emotionally secure and resilient person.

Sometimes people who are disconnected from their true nature or who don't have a positive view of themselves can take out their painful lack of self-worth on other people. They might bring others down as a way of feeling better about themselves, or they may project their feelings of inadequacy onto others, becoming overly critical and judgemental. If you recognise any of those patterns within yourself, it's essential that you take responsibility for healing the wounds that are keeping you from developing positive and supportive relationships with other people. And if you're on the receiving end of those behaviours, part of your own healing is to have enough self-respect to stop tolerating them.

BE YOURSELF

Have you ever spent some time with someone, but felt like you never really knew them? Maybe you have conversations that never go deeper than surface level, or they're so quick to agree with your point of view that you're not sure if you're hearing their real opinion, or even if they have an opinion at all. Those people are awfully hard to connect with. It feels like you're tapping on the window but never getting to talk to the real person inside.

I had a friend once who projected an image of confidence when I first met her. As we got to know each other better, I began to notice, first in subtle ways and then in glaringly obvious ones, that any preference or decision I shared, she quickly adopted as her own. From career choices to holiday destinations or even what to serve dinner guests, everything I did, she also did. What was disconcerting about this was that she never acknowledged it, which made me feel like I might have been imagining it. If she'd said to me, 'I'd never thought about doing that. Great idea. You really inspired me', it would have been flattering and appreciated.

But having the sense that someone is quietly taking notes on your life and presenting all your ideas as their own is weird and creepy. Other behaviours made it clear (not surprisingly) that she suffered from very low self-esteem and a constant need to prove herself, but sadly, she went about that in very self-defeating ways.

When you know who you are and what you value, and you feel comfortable in your own skin despite any perceived flaws you might have, you're able to bring your real, authentic and imperfect self to your relationships with other people. And when you bring your whole self, you're more likely to attract people into your life who also value and appreciate you. Posturing and pretending is not the path to authentic connection.

If you're not the most confident person, or if you struggle with poor self-image, being willing to share that in an honest way is much more likely to build trust and rapport than putting on a facade. As an added benefit, the more willing you are to be vulnerable, the more likely others are to drop their own mask. When you're real, you're relatable, and so much more likeable.

WHO ARE YOU AND WHAT DO YOU WANT?

What are your values? So many people struggle to answer that question. What are the qualities you admire most in other people? Is it their compassion? Grit? Humour? What are the qualities you admire most in yourself? Courage? Creativity? Integrity? At your 90th birthday party when your loved ones give a speech in your honour, what would you want them to say are your most outstanding personal qualities or notable achievements?

On a more everyday level, what topics of conversation get you excited and what bores you to tears? What kind of books do you like to read (or do you prefer audiobooks)? Which movies or TV shows do you love? What breaks your heart in the world? Where do you stand on organised religion? Politics? Spirituality? Do you have a strong opinion either way?

When you spend time reflecting on who you are and what matters most to you, a couple of interesting things happen. First of all, tapping into your values and strengths, your type of humour, the things you're naturally good at, what qualities you most admire in yourself and others, your goals in life, and what you can appreciate about yourself (despite all your imperfections), you start to build a solid sense of yourself as a person of character and substance.

Secondly, this means that if you find yourself being pulled down the old well-worn path of self-criticism because you don't like your weight or your hair or some aspect of your personality, you now have something a lot deeper and more meaningful to connect with. Your core values, integrity, kindness, the things that inspire and excite you – these are the qualities you bring to any relationship, and these are the traits worth focusing your attention on.

TAMING YOUR INNER CRITIC

We all have aspects of ourselves we don't love; in fact, most of us are highly self-critical. Maybe you're socially awkward or a bit hot-headed. Perhaps there are aspects of your appearance you wish were different. Maybe you're constantly comparing yourself to other people and you've decided they are infinitely more organised, disciplined and successful than you.

Our brains are wired to default to negative self-talk if they have nothing else to focus on. We have a strong negativity bias, which is designed to keep us safe, and that old social brain of ours is very concerned with focusing on ourselves and imagining how other people might be judging us. This is not something that can be easily turned off, but it can be managed. When you're so heavily focused on all the things you perceive to be wrong with you, it's hard to tap into those positive qualities and cultivate feelings of warmth, friendliness and patience towards yourself.

People who struggle with self-acceptance often have no problem extending kindness to others. They're generous, endlessly patient and self-sacrificing.

They acknowledge that they find it easier to express compassion for others than for themselves. They *genuinely* don't believe that their lack of self-kindness has any impact on their capacity to create balanced and healthy relationships with others. In fact, they sometimes think their willingness to set aside their own needs in order to be available to others is what makes them a good friend or partner. I beg to differ.

Ideally, people will value you and treat you with the kindness you deserve simply for being you. But if they don't, how would you know to stand up for yourself if you don't believe you deserve any better? How much more difficult would that be for you if you have an unhelpful schema running in the background, or an insecure attachment style?

UNLEARNING SELF-CRITICISM

While self-criticism is a natural human tendency that we all experience to some degree, a lot of the things we get down on ourselves for are actually learned. When you were a baby learning to walk, you didn't waste an ounce of your exuberant energy comparing yourself to the toddler down the street who was off and running. You weren't concerned about singing off key when you belted out the alphabet song. You certainly didn't wonder if you should lay off the egg custard when you squished your chubby thighs between your fat fingers.

Slowly, as we grow from infancy to childhood, adolescence and then adulthood, we start absorbing the drip-feed of messages from the world about what's expected, what's appropriate and, most importantly, what's going to get us validation and approval. We first learn from our immediate family how we need to behave. Without even knowing it we're also internalising the social and cultural messages that tell us what's expected, and we start forming conclusions about all the ways we're not good enough.

There are some fairly pervasive gender stereotypes that form part of that social conditioning, which is almost impossible to escape. Typically, little girls learn that sharing, being quiet and playing nicely are positive attributes that win you a lot of praise. We girls learn that how we look is one of our most important qualities. We observe that the ideal woman is attractive, thin, feminine, kind, nurturing and self-sacrificing.

Boys learn that being strong and brave are positive attributes. Men are providers, they're emotionally tough and can't be seen as weak. Even in families where both (heterosexual) parents work, surveys consistently show that it's mothers who handle the bulk of the housework, carry the mental load, and do the vast majority of parenting on top of their day job.

So what's all this got to do with relationships? Well, based on all those internalised messages, it's easy to fall into the trap of measuring our worth against social values and expectations. If I'm an ambitious and driven woman, maybe I need to tone it down a little. Do friends and colleagues find me too aggressive? What if

I scare people off? As a man, if I'm earning less than my partner, will they respect me? If I show my emotion or reveal vulnerability, will they think I'm pathetic?

We start to downplay what we consider to be the unappealing parts of our personality and pretend to be something else as a way of fitting in and being accepted. We diminish our own needs to accommodate others' expectations. We betray and abandon ourselves rather than stepping fully into who we're meant to be.

The goal here is not to become a self-absorbed narcissist who steamrolls everyone in your path while you focus on getting your own needs met. It's simply for you to recognise all the ways you might be holding yourself back from fully expressing who you are, and starting to do the work of being comfortable in your skin, confident of your value, and willing to treat your own authentic needs, wants, desires, preferences and opinions with as much respect as you do others'. I'd like you to extend to yourself the same compassion, friendliness and patience that you offer to your friends, family and perhaps even strangers. I want you to know deeply that you are as worthy of *your own* love and acceptance.

If you feel your needs aren't being met in friendships or romantic relationships, the only way to change your outer world is for you to transform yourself from the inside out. When you respect yourself, you command respect from others. You bring the best out of yourself and you bring out the best in others. As you grow to becoming the truest, happiest version of yourself, you elevate everyone who comes into contact with you, and become a magnet for high-quality relationships with people who are healthy and whole.

TO KNOW YOU IS TO LOVE YOU

Connect with your values

Spend some time reflecting on what's important to you. This is not only important for building your own self-awareness and boosting your self-esteem, it also helps you to more quickly identify and attract the people who are likely to be a good fit for you. Shared values are one of the most important ingredients for a lasting connection.

Identify your strengths

One of the most effective ways to increase feelings of self-worth and challenge self-criticism is to affirm your strengths. These are the qualities that you appreciate most about yourself, and might include your particular gifts, talents or personal attributes. If you have trouble identifying your strengths, try asking some of your friends and family to find out what they appreciate most about you. You might be surprised by the gifts others see in you.

Honour your needs

If you typically put your own needs last or act as if you don't have needs at all, start making time regularly to look after yourself. Treat your desires and preferences as equally important as other people's. This might mean taking time out to rest, to be alone or to pursue a personal ambition or goal. Act like you matter.

Step five

MAKE
MEANINGFUL
CONNECTIONS

Most of the people who move in and out of your life are there by chance, not because of any deliberate action or intention.

You end up working in the same office together, your kids go to the same school or your partners share an interest. There are perhaps hundreds of people in your extended social network with whom you share only a very loose connection.

Sometimes you bond with someone for a brief period by virtue of those shared circumstances. You're assigned to work on a project together or you realise you share a mutual dislike of the boss. The frequency or intensity of your communication may increase temporarily, but when circumstances change and you realise there's nothing more substantial to hold you together, you go your separate ways.

Occasionally though, one of those random connections develops into something deeper, and you realise there's an opportunity to form a more enduring alliance. But to progress a relationship through all the stages from casual acquaintance to genuinely close, lasting friend requires intentional effort and some specific ingredients.

THREE INGREDIENTS FOR CONNECTION

Shasta Nelson is a friendship expert and author of the books *Friendships Don't Just Happen* and *Frientimacy*. She makes the point that if you feel you're lacking intimacy or closeness, the solution is usually not to add more people to the mix; most of us can pull out our phones and have instant access to daily updates from hundreds of 'friends' online. Rather, it's the quality of those connections that determines whether we're left wanting for more. Nelson's research found that there are three primary ingredients that all relationships must have if they're to satisfy our deep need for connection: consistency, positivity and vulnerability.

Consistency

One important ingredient necessary for connections to develop and flourish is time. It's the consistency of interaction and time spent getting to know each other that allows a relationship to evolve from casual acquaintance to genuine friend, and ultimately to trusted confidant. Of course, this explains why so many of our lasting relationships spring up in places like school and work. Showing up every day in the same place covers the requirement for consistency.

Having said that, there are obviously some people who will never become anything more than a casual contact, no matter how much time you spend together. For friendship intimacy to be a possibility, there need to be shared values and common interests, but it's only with consistency that you have the opportunity to dig deep enough to reveal the common ground.

Positivity

We connect with people who are open and friendly, and when there is an overall positive tone to your interaction. We naturally gravitate towards people who we feel good around. Kindness, a willingness to listen and a warm smile are alluring qualities. If you spend a lot of time with someone who is typically pessimistic, complaining or unpleasant to be around – for example, if they're impatient, rude or constantly fault-finding – you're unlikely to feel enthusiastic about deepening your connection. You want to be with people who elevate your mood and bring out the best in you.

With consistent interaction and an overall tone of positivity, a deeper connection can take root and begin to grow. But if the conversation is always positive, the tone is always upbeat and it doesn't feel like there's space in the relationship to share anything challenging or personal, you might still feel like something is missing.

"With consistent interaction and an overall tone of positivity, a deeper connection can take root and begin to grow."

Vulnerability

The third ingredient necessary for any relationship to move beyond the superficial to a more intimate connection is vulnerability. When you share something of yourself that is personal, you are trusting someone with a part of you that is precious, and you're giving them an opportunity to demonstrate that they are trustworthy. Vulnerability can mean sharing your struggles as well as your joy. When you open yourself up to a conversation that goes a little deeper than superficialities, such as when you talk about your goals in life or details about your family, you invite the other person to do the same. It's in this sharing back and forth, slowly peeling back the layers to reveal more intimate aspects of yourself and your life, that you build high-quality, trusting and satisfying connections.

IMPROVING YOUR CONNECTIONS

The three essential ingredients to friendship intimacy provide a nice starting point for assessing the health of your current social network. If you feel like something is missing, it might be that you have lots of relationships that are positive and vulnerable, but they're suffering from a lack of consistent contact. Can you set up a regular monthly brunch or phone call? Maybe you have a great friend who's going through some hard stuff, so there's consistent, vulnerable sharing, but the friendship has lost its positivity. In that case, perhaps you need to seek out some light and fun conversation with a different person to balance the equation.

When there is a gap between the level of friendship intimacy you crave and what you actually experience, there are practical and meaningful steps you can take to improve the quality of your connections. This starts with identifying precisely which need isn't being met.

QUALITY OVER QUANTITY

Social media and smartphones have certainly expanded our capacity for connection. There's no limit to the number of 'friends' you can have in your online world but, according to anthropologist Robin Dunbar, there is a limit to the number of people with whom we can form meaningful connections. Dunbar's theory is that while you might recognise up to 1500 faces, you can only have *meaningful* relationships with 150 people. Within that 150, there are expanding concentric circles representing different levels of intimacy.

Inside your inner circle you have only three to five loved ones. These are the people you would call on in a crisis. Sadly, some surveys have revealed that many struggle to name even one person they could count on. You don't need a lot of friends, but you do need to know that there are at least a few people who truly see you and will be there for you.

BE THE FRIEND YOU WANT TO HAVE

When you have the basics for a meaningful and nourishing friendship, the best way to deepen and strengthen that alliance is to be the friend you'd like someone to be to you. We all know what that looks like. It's proving yourself to be a trustworthy person by never breaching someone's confidence, and showing yourself to be a person of integrity by following through on your promises and keeping commitments. It's being loyal and having someone's back. You know the friends you can count on will be the ones who defend you when you're not there to defend yourself.

When you're in someone's company, make eye contact and put down your phone. Nothing tells a person they don't matter like responding to text messages while they're trying to have a conversation with you. Being a good friend means making an effort to remember important dates or details. It's small, thoughtful gestures like remembering that someone's mum was having surgery and checking in to see how it went.

Most of us think of great friends as the ones who are there to support us in the hard times, and it's true – those people are angels. But the best kinds of friends are the ones who equally share your joy and celebrate your success. 'Mudita' is a Pali word from the Buddhist tradition that means 'sympathetic joy'. It means expressing your genuine and heartfelt enthusiasm when someone shares with you their happy news, whether it be a job promotion, pregnancy or lucky windfall. The truly special friend puts aside any feelings of envy or competition and celebrates with you. Less worthy friends will downplay your news, change the subject, focus on how it affects them or find something negative. Be the person who offers Mudita when your friend has a win.

MAKING NEW FRIENDS

There are times in life when we actually *do* need to make new friends. People move away, get married, have kids. Interests diverge, and friendships fizzle out. If you've ever found yourself in that situation, you'll have quickly learned that making friends as an adult is nowhere near as easy as it was when we were kids.

An added complication is that admitting you're lonely or that you don't have a wide circle of friends can create feelings of shame. Somehow, despite the fact that loneliness is an epidemic (and the stats are right there to prove it), we assume we're the only ones struggling, and that our lack of friends is a reflection on our likeability or worthiness. That stigma stops us from reaching out and making an effort to forge new connections. Given how critical relationships are to our health and happiness, it's imperative that we get over our discomfort and fear of rejection and make a conscious, intentional effort to build new networks. According to one study of friendship, we need to spend around 50 hours with someone before we reach a comfortable level of familiarity, and close friendships develop after spending about 200 hours together. Cultivating friendships takes time, and as we all know, time is a finite resource in our busy lives. Therefore, if you find yourself with a friendship gap, it can be a good idea to start by reconnecting with old friends. Most of us have a long list of people who were close friends once, but the quality of those relationships has diminished purely due to busyness and a lack of regular contact. Usually, those relationships have already benefited from a significant investment of time, so it doesn't take much to rekindle the connection.

New connections are often built on shared interests, so joining groups (even online ones) or attending events in your local area can be a great way to meet people who share your interests. The benefit of a specific interest group, whether it's bushwalking or tarot card reading or even your kid's sports event, is that there's immediately a mutual interest and something to talk about.

When you meet someone new, it takes time to move that connection from casual acquaintance to friend, to close friend. That process is helped along by a willingness to invest your time and energy in getting to know them better. We often feel awkward and self-conscious engaging in small talk, and worry about what other people think of us, but you can avoid that discomfort by showing interest in the other person and taking the spotlight off yourself. Ask people about themselves and then really listen to their answers. Point out the things you have in common.

If someone expresses an interest in getting to know you better or you meet someone who has great friend potential, extend invitations and create opportunities to spend more time together. I also recommend being very specific about your availability. We're all so accustomed to saying, 'Oh we must catch up' and then never following up with a concrete plan. If you're able to tell someone, 'Great. I'm usually free most nights except Thursday, and weekends are good for me', this signals your sincerity and encourages the other person to think more specifically about their own availability.

YOU CAN'T FAST-TRACK CONNECTION

Connection is founded on authenticity and the willingness to drop your mask and be vulnerable, but too much vulnerability can backfire. Sometimes it's inauthentic and contrived to fast-track trust. Sometimes it's too much, too soon. If someone over-shares intimate details of their life very soon after meeting you, it can feel like a boundary has been violated. It's an unfair burden to be privy to someone's personal

"Sometimes it's inauthentic and contrived to fast-track trust. Sometimes it's too much, too soon."

information before you've had the chance to work out if they're a person you want that kind of connection with. These are examples of what Brené Brown refers to as 'hot-wiring' connection.

Another damaging approach to forging connection is using gossip as a path to camaraderie. When you bond with someone over your mutual dislike of someone else, it breeds toxicity and negativity, and ultimately it erodes trust. When someone gossips to you about another person, part of you is registering that this person would just as easily gossip about you. And as harsh as it may be, that's also the message you're conveying when you demonstrate that you're willing to talk about someone else behind their back.

TAKE IT OFFLINE

These days we do most of our communicating via smartphone or social media. It's convenient, efficient and, as we've recently discovered, can be a godsend during a global pandemic. But if you have the option to see someone face to face, and talk to them with your voice, not via text on a screen, those are the kinds of interactions that allow for more depth of connection.

Social media, as we all know, presents a highlights reel of our life, and even if we share our challenges online, it's a two-dimensional snapshot of real life. Online messaging doesn't allow for tone of voice, gestures or facial expressions. Real connection happens when we make the time in our lives to really see people. The very act of making the time demonstrates a level of commitment and investment in the relationship, and that's one of the most important ingredients for meaningful connection.

MAKE IT MEANINGFUL

Do a friendship health check

You might want to do a little audit of your social connections and see where you can inject some positivity, consistency or vulnerability to add depth and increase satisfaction in your existing friendships. How many of your friends would you feel comfortable to call on in a crisis or share a personal struggle with? We don't need a lot of friends but it's important we have a trusted few.

Remember the little things

In our busy lives, it's often the small gestures that
create the most lasting impact. Take note of birthdays
and anniversaries, pay attention to the details of
someone's life and their work and family. Follow up.
Ask how they're going. Intimacy is found in sharing the
day-to-day details of our lives.

Be happy for other people's happiness

When anyone trusts you with their good news, allow your enthusiasm to be unbridled. Jump for joy, ask them for more details, express your delight and let them talk about it as much as they want. Sympathetic joy is the sign of a real, loyal and genuine friend.

Step six

TAKE RESPONSIBILITY

By now, it should be abundantly clear that we each bring our own complex personal history and unique life experiences to our relationships.

We each have distinct personalities, interests, values, preferences and communication styles. Not everyone sees the world the same way you do. Not everyone has the same need for emotional reassurance or physical space. Not everyone is as comfortable with expressing emotions. Not everyone lives by the same rules. None of us can be responsible for someone else's behaviour, perceptions or experiences. What we must each take responsibility for is how effectively we communicate, how willing we are to own our part in our relationships, and the effort we make to understand and appreciate differences.

In healthy, satisfying and emotionally mature relationships, there is the expectation that each person will offer something of themselves and that they'll derive some benefit in return. We give and receive companionship, conversation, emotional support, advice, laughter and love. We offer our time and attention, and in return we gain all the social, emotional and physiological advantages that come from having a meaningful connection. In order for a relationship to survive and thrive, we each have to hold up our end of the bargain.

"What we must each take responsibility for is how effectively we communicate, how willing we are to own our part in our relationships, and the effort we make to understand and appreciate differences."

WHEN THINGS ARE OUT OF BALANCE

As relationships evolve, there may be periods when one person needs more support than the other. If someone is going through a difficult period, the giving and receiving might not be split equally, but that's the nature of relationships. They're fluid and dynamic, not fixed and static. Sometimes though, that off-balance, 'more give than take' dynamic isn't temporary. In some relationships, it can feel like you're doing all the work, making all the effort and always compromising to accommodate the other person.

Conversely, in some relationships maybe you're the one who makes no effort. You wait for your friend to call you, but you never initiate the communication. You're not that into someone, but you carry on a half-hearted relationship because there's no-one else more appealing on your radar. Whether you are the giver or the taker in this equation, my advice is the same: it's time to step up. If you know you're on the receiving end of poor treatment, it's your responsibility to either communicate your expectations or extricate yourself from the situation. If you're the one taking advantage, you might want to consider whether you're acting in line with your values.

I think it's important to make one small caveat to this advice. We all have a tendency to only see situations from our own perspective. Most of us can easily identify all the ways we contribute in any situation, but don't necessarily see or appreciate all the different ways someone else is making an effort. You may perceive that you're the one doing all the giving, but your friend may well have an entirely different view. It's important to keep an open mind and be willing to have honest conversations with people, not only to express how you're feeling but to be willing to understand someone else's experience.

ACT WITH INTEGRITY

How often have you said to someone that you really must catch up and then six months later you still haven't made any plans? Have you ever felt annoyed or let down by a friend and chosen to vent to a third party rather than speaking openly and honestly to the person who hurt you? Perhaps you've got an inkling that you might have unintentionally hurt someone else's feelings, but instead of apologising or attempting to rectify the situation, you decided that since you didn't mean it, it's their problem to deal with. If you ignore it, hopefully it will go away.

We've all been on one side or the other of these small transgressions. Rather than taking responsibility for clearing up any misunderstandings, telling the truth about how we feel or following through on our promises, we just let them slip by, hoping that with time they'll be forgotten. We tell ourselves that these things happen, we all get busy, they'll get over it or we'll get over it. In the scheme of things, it doesn't really matter.

In our endlessly busy lives, it's easy to let our reliance on technology and social media reduce the

quality of our conversations. We don't have time for long chats on the phone, but we can shoot off a quick text message and tell ourselves we kept in touch.
It's a token gesture really, and a poor substitute for meaningful connection. At the end of the day, we can make excuses or we can take responsibility for the decisions and actions we make, which either support connection or slowly erode it.

High-quality relationships are based on a foundation of trust and experts agree that trust is built in small moments, not grand gestures. No matter how busy you are, it's the choice you make in those small moments to either turn towards someone or to keep your head down and keep moving that make all the difference to the quality of your relationships.

TAKE RESPONSIBILITY FOR YOUR OWN HAPPINESS

When you're feeling dissatisfied with the quality of your relationships, it's easy to look outside yourself for the source of the problem. We slip into blame when we feel hurt, and we can always find ways to justify our own feelings and reactions. You might tell yourself that if only *they* would do something different, treat you better or listen to you more closely, everything would be fine. If only they hadn't done that thing or made that choice, if only they would spend more time with you, you wouldn't feel sad or lonely. Couldn't they just make more effort to anticipate your needs and accommodate your wishes?

The problem with making your happiness contingent upon someone else's choices and actions is that it is utterly disempowering. I know there have been times in my own life when I've allowed my mood to be affected by the mood of those around me. You can probably recall times when you have too.

Early in my marriage, I used to feel frustrated if my husband was in a bad mood. I would try to support him, but also I'd feel annoyed because of how it affected me, especially if I wanted to go out and do something and he wasn't interested. Eventually, I learned that his mood is not my responsibility, and nor is it his job to 'snap out of it' to make me happy. His feelings are his. Mine are entirely my own. Being responsible for your own happiness means sometimes making your own plans, rather than sulking or feeling resentful. It most certainly means not making yourself a victim of other people's choices.

It's important to note here that choosing to take responsibility for your own happiness doesn't mean pasting on a smile while you tolerate someone else's bad behaviour. Sometimes taking responsibility means clearly communicating your expectations, setting limits, holding firm boundaries and making the choice to remove someone from your life if it's clear the relationship is not in your best interests.

My friend Ava fell in love with a guy who was everything she'd dreamed of. He'd been through many life challenges and now had a career as a motivational speaker and coach. She loved his passion and his positive attitude. What he taught in seminars was the power of choosing your own response in any given situation. Ava had learned this life lesson firsthand, having suffered the tragic loss of her husband some years earlier. She couldn't have been happier to meet someone who lived by the values she too held dear. But soon after they moved in together, she began to see another side to him. He would fly into a rage over the smallest things. When she told him that what she wanted in their relationship was harmony, he told her what he tells everyone – that experiencing peace and harmony was her choice, and that her happiness was her responsibility. He, on the other hand, took no responsibility for his actions. It took a long time for Ava to realise she was in a relationship with a narcissist, and she eventually found the courage to leave.

If you find yourself in a relationship with someone who is volatile, passive aggressive or dishonest, or who belittles you, is condescending or causes you to question your confidence, this is not a sign that you need to work on yourself. These are bright red flags signalling that you should get out of this situation. And while you most definitely will benefit from some self-reflection, looking closely and compassionately at what drew you to this person, I suggest you do that work after you have extricated yourself from the situation, when you are in an emotionally and physically safe place.

Taking responsibility
for your happiness
also means not
tolerating abuse.

YOU'RE ONLY RESPONSIBLE FOR YOU

When you care about someone, it's natural to want what's best for them. Of course, any relationship involves compromise. Sometimes we choose to put someone else's needs or priorities ahead of our own.

A sign of a healthy relationship and a characteristic of a secure attachment is interdependence. This means that both people feel comfortable depending on each other as well as being independent. They both prioritise the relationship, but equally are able to enjoy time and interests outside of it. They're each willing to communicate and negotiate so that they both have their needs met.

Problems arise when one person in a relationship only feels happy and safe when the other person is okay. Being willing to take full responsibility for someone else's happiness and for them getting their needs met could be a sign of co-dependence. The term co-dependent was originally used to describe partners of addicts, but these days is used to describe any relationship in which one person feels completely responsible for the other person's happiness, while the other person takes no ownership and possibly even blames their partner for their problems. There are no healthy boundaries in place.

The term co-dependent refers to the fact that each person depends on the other in an unhealthy way. One person needs the other person to take care of them. The 'care-taker' needs to be needed. Co-dependency can be found in friendships, romantic relationships and families.

Remember, you are responsible for your choices, your behaviour, and how you manage your own emotions. You are responsible for your communication and you are responsible for the energy you bring to your interactions. You're also absolutely responsible for the kind of energy you allow others to bring. If you're self-sacrificing, people pleasing, enabling someone's dysfunctional behaviour or assuming responsibility for someone else's mental health issues, this is a sign that you need to step back and take care of yourself.

TAKE GOOD CARE OF YOUR RELATIONSHIPS

Make the effort

We can all come up with endless reasons why we've been too busy to see people or to have important conversations. We can let people fade out of our lives and tell ourselves it's not our fault. Taking full responsibility is not the easy option but it's the right one, and it's the one most likely to result in relationships that grow deeper and stronger with time.

Stay out of the blame game

If I'm feeling like I want to blame others for how I'm feeling, I find a really helpful question to ask is, 'Where am I angry at myself?' I can almost always trace at least part of the problem back to me. Maybe I haven't communicated my expectations clearly, or I didn't speak up about something when I had the chance. Even if someone else has done the wrong thing, you'll gain a much more balanced view when you look within and own your part.

Hold your line

One of the most important aspects of taking responsibility is knowing where you end and another person begins. Draw a solid line around your time, space, energy, money, emotions, thoughts and feelings. Own what's yours. Let go of everything that isn't.

Step seven

SET HEALTHY
BOUNDARIES

Boundaries are the limits you set, which define what you consider to be the reasonable, acceptable ways for other people to behave towards you and also for you to behave towards others.

In other words, they're bi-directional, affecting both your incoming and outgoing interactions.

Where there are clear boundaries, there's integrity. Personal integrity is living a life where your outer actions are in alignment with your inner thoughts and feelings. Therefore, in order to set clear boundaries, you need to be in touch with your inner world – your values, needs, opinions, desires, preferences and the physical sensations that alert you to what feels right and what doesn't.

Setting boundaries requires you to know what matters to you and to trust your own judgement and be guided by your own inner knowing, rather than by outside influences. When you're in touch with your inner wisdom, it will steer you towards what's in your best interest. If you've spent your life paying more attention to other people's needs and preferences, it can take time to learn how to trust yourself to know what's right for you.

Boundaries can be both physical and psychological. Your physical boundaries determine how much personal space you need, the kind of physical touch that's comfortable for you and the level of privacy you expect. Your psychological or emotional boundaries reflect the degree to which you take responsibility for your own thoughts and feelings, and how willing you are to *not* take responsibility for other people's. You can set boundaries around your time, your money and your energy.

WHAT DO HEALTHY BOUNDARIES LOOK LIKE?

While many people talk about the importance of setting and maintaining boundaries, it's not always clear how to actually do that. How do you know if your boundaries are too soft or too rigid? When is it appropriate to be flexible with those boundaries and when do you need to stay firm? And the biggest question that I hear: How do I communicate my boundaries without hurting someone's feelings or creating conflict?

If a friend is pressuring you to go out and you've been looking forward to a quiet night at home, being firm with your boundaries means being prepared to disappoint your friend in order to be true to yourself and honour your needs. If a family member is prying into your personal affairs, your boundaries might mean you choose to not engage in that discussion, even if it feels awkward or rude. Asserting your boundaries might also mean pointing out to someone that you found their comment offensive rather than letting it slide – for example, if they made a racist joke or sexist remark.

It's about acting outwardly in a way that is congruent with what's happening inwardly.

When your boundaries are too soft, you'll have trouble asserting your own needs and preferences and can end up feeling exhausted and resentful. You might stay too long in an unsatisfying relationship because you don't want to hurt someone's feelings, or take on too many commitments because you have trouble saying no, and you probably feel overly responsible for other people's happiness. People pleasing is a sign of blurred boundaries because it's often an outward manifestation of an inner desire to avoid someone else's judgement or criticism.

Unclear boundaries can also cause you to carry the emotional weight of other people's problems as if they're your own, or you may be overly invested in trying to 'fix' someone rather than allowing them to exercise their own free will. Earlier, we discussed co-dependence as an example of this kind of boundary violation. In the reverse, you might be on the receiving end of other people's efforts to try to fix or save you, rather than being empowered to take personal responsibility for your life.

If your boundaries are too rigid, you might have trouble letting people get too close to you. You might be unwilling to ask for or receive offers of help. Rigid boundaries sometimes come about because you've been hurt in the past and you fear too much intimacy (perhaps you might now see links between an avoidant attachment style or an emotional deprivation type schema). Rigid, impenetrable boundaries can lead to chronic feelings of loneliness and isolation.

HOW TO SET HEALTHY BOUNDARIES

The first step to setting healthy boundaries is knowing who you are, what you stand for and what you're willing (and therefore unwilling) to tolerate. This means you can only create clear and firm boundaries when you know what matters most to you, are comfortable with who you are and are willing to take responsibility for yourself.

Boundaries can be tricky if you've grown up in an environment where you felt that your needs and opinions weren't treated as important or valid, or if you received approval for putting other people's feelings and opinions ahead of your own. Again, you might notice direct links between soft boundaries and having a subjugation or self-sacrifice schema. If you grew up in a family environment where everyone was overly involved in each other's personal affairs or there was a lack of respect for each family member's right to privacy and personal space, it can feel uncomfortable trying to determine and enforce your boundaries as an adult.

Your boundaries are often a reflection of your values.

As children, we often aren't taught the skills of assertiveness. In fact, we're often encouraged to smile and be polite, to mind our manners, respect our elders or even to show affection to relative strangers. As adults, we can carry those programmed responses with us, and therefore feel obligated to make sure we don't offend someone, even if that means we create discomfort for ourselves. That's why learning to set and express your boundaries might feel uncomfortable at first. But remember, boundaries can be flexible. It's not about being uncompromising, or saying no to every request.

The good news is that when two people are each very clear about their personal boundaries and are comfortable expressing them, everyone knows where they stand. Having that degree of clarity about the expectations on both sides allows relationships to flow with ease, because it removes any confusion, second guessing or ambiguity. You don't have to like someone else's boundary, but you can appreciate knowing exactly where their lines are drawn. It's a win-win for everyone involved.

LOOK FOR RED FLAGS

Sometimes you realise there are people in your life who aren't interested in honouring your boundaries. They're more take than give, they provoke you into arguments, take advantage of your good nature, don't support your decisions or goals, or cause you to doubt yourself.

Some people are narcissistic. A narcissist lacks empathy, has a strong sense of entitlement and has no problem exploiting others for their own gain. If your boundaries get in the way of a narcissist's goals, they will be ignored. Narcissists also have a way of causing you to question yourself, or convincing you that you're the problem. They are particularly drawn to people who have a lot of empathy and compassion, so they can be very intimidating to deal with. When dealing with a narcissist, sometimes the only option is to cut all contact.

Some people are skilled in the art of emotional blackmail. An emotional blackmailer will use a lot of manipulative strategies to get you to compromise your boundaries. They'll say things like, 'If you really loved me …', 'You obviously don't care …', 'After all I've done for you …', or 'I'll leave you if …'. Holding firm to your boundaries is especially challenging when you're dealing with someone who is manipulative, but in these cases it's particularly important that you hold your line, seek support and remove those people from your life.

SIMPLE STEPS TO SETTING BOUNDARIES

Learn to say no

If you have trouble saying no because you're worried about hurting someone or letting them down, remember, this is a skill that can be learned. The important thing, once you're clear on your boundaries, is to tolerate the discomfort that you feel when you need to enforce them. This can mean taking a deep breath and observing any feelings of worry or guilt without letting your behaviour be dictated by those feelings. You might practise saying, 'Let me get back to you' or 'I'll have to check my calendar' before giving a firm answer. Buy yourself some time so you don't feel pressured to agree to something you may later regret.

Pay attention to what drains you

Are there particular people in your life who leave you feeling depleted after you spend time with them? Pay attention to those signals. Are there activities you've committed to that no longer give you any feeling of positivity? Does a regular family activity fill you with dread? These are all signs that you're neglecting or ignoring your own needs. It's important to create some boundaries around your time and energy.

Take a purposeful pause

When you feel an urge to say yes to an engagement, volunteer to help out a friend or invite someone to stay at your house instead of a hotel, pause for a moment and take a deep breath. Ask yourself if this is what you really want, or if you're acting out of a sense of obligation or doing what you think is expected. Sit with the feeling for a while before you commit, and practise flexing those boundary muscles. You'll soon become more comfortable defining your own limits.

Step eight

HANDLE
CONFLICT
LIKE A PRO

Relationships are messy.

Inevitably, if you spend enough time in another person's company, you're going to experience a miscommunication or disagreement. Feelings get hurt, expectations aren't met, harsh words are spoken, or someone feels let down.

The goal of any relationship is not to avoid disagreements altogether; in fact, that can be a sign of a particularly unhealthy dynamic. What's most important, and most likely to determine whether your partnership lasts the distance, is how you choose to manage conflict when it arises.

MANAGING CONFLICT

John Gottman is a world-renowned couples therapist and researcher who can predict, with stunning accuracy, whether a couple is likely to divorce after watching them discuss a heated topic for just 15 minutes. Based on his observations of thousands of couples, he's identified three styles of conflict management, which can all result in lasting, happy relationships. You might be relieved to know that couples who argue frequently can survive and thrive, and so can 'conflict minimisers' (some might call them conflict avoiders!). And while some couples may be more proficient in the skilful communication normally associated with successful relationships, those skills aren't essential for a relationship to succeed.

The three distinct conflict management styles have been called validating, volatile and avoidant.

Validating

Validators are probably what most of us would think of as the 'ideal' conflict managers. They're the ultimate communicators, discussing issues calmly, listening attentively, acknowledging each other's points of view and always focusing on the issue at hand rather than resorting to personal attacks. It's no surprise that they tend to enjoy long, happy and satisfying relationships.

Volatile

The volatile couple is more likely to engage in heated, passionate debates. They argue frequently, and often over small things. They have a very high level of engagement, and when the relationship works well it's because they bring that same level of intensity and commitment to the positive parts of their relationship, including love, affection and laughter.

Avoidant

Ah, the conflict minimisers. Avoidant people conveniently skirt around contentious issues, downplay the significance of differences and agree to disagree. What seems to work is that they choose to put their attention on where they're compatible, rather than focus on differences. They don't sweat the small things. It might not be the most passionate relationship, but there's a lot of stability and security.

It turns out that the way you argue is less important than whether you both bring the same approach to resolving differences. What doesn't work so well is if you have, for example, one person who is volatile and another who is avoidant. It's not that those relationship dynamics can't work. They just require an extra level of understanding, empathy and a willingness to compromise.

My friend Julie grew up in a close-knit family in Australia and can't recall there ever being any outward conflict between her parents or siblings. In her early twenties, while backpacking around Europe, she met Marco, a fiery young Italian who had grown up with a very different family dynamic and culture. Early in their relationship, Julie realised that Marco loves nothing more than to passionately (loudly) thrash out a debate. Julie, on the other hand, had no experience of this. While Marco's style of arguing was unsettling at first, she realised that her own family's more subdued approach might not have been the healthiest either. The good news for Julie is that, coming from such a secure family home, she was not lacking in self-confidence or self-worth, and so the power dynamic between the two of them was balanced. She recognised that she simply needed to learn how to use her voice and argue her point. Someone with a less secure attachment style may have had a very different experience. They're happily married and still managing to resolve their differences twenty years later.

DESTRUCTIVE COMMUNICATION

When providing relationship counselling, one of the first things I always shared with distressed couples was what Gottman calls the 'Four Horsemen of the Apocalypse'. These are the patterns of communication most likely to sabotage any relationship. I believe they're as destructive in platonic and family relationships as they are for couples. All of us should be on the lookout for the four horsemen creeping into our conversations. They are criticism, contempt, defensiveness and stonewalling.

Criticism

Criticism is more of an attack on the person or their character than a specific complaint about an unwanted behaviour. For example, the complaint, 'It bothers me that you spend money unnecessarily when we agreed to save' might turn into, 'You're so irresponsible with money!' Criticism often involves making generalisations such as 'You always ...' or

'You never …', rather than focusing on the specific issue at hand. Criticism is hurtful and destructive for obvious reasons, although if we're honest, we probably all slip into criticism occasionally.

Contempt

If there's a lot of criticism between two people, this can grow into contempt. Contempt might be as subtle as a dismissive eye-roll, or it can be expressed as open hostility, name-calling and insults. Contempt is nasty. It's hurtful and disrespectful. Where there's contempt there is little room for kindness, empathy or compromise.

Defensiveness

Being defensive when under attack is a very natural human response. The problem with defensiveness is that it's so focused on self-protection it stops listening for the truth, and leaves no room for open, healthy dialogue. When the dynamics of a relationship cause you to feel emotionally unsafe, you're unlikely to make yourself open and vulnerable, but if you find yourself being defensive at even the slightest complaint from someone, it's important to learn to receive feedback without resorting to justifications, excuses or counterattacks. Healthy relationships thrive on open, non-defensive airing of grievances.

Stonewalling

Stonewalling is the complete disengagement from any communication. It's giving someone the silent treatment or walking out and refusing to enter into any kind of meaningful dialogue. There is no talking to a brick wall, so if one person is stonewalling another, it's hard to make any positive progress. If one person has a habit of stonewalling, perhaps because of an avoidant attachment, this is an indication that there's work to be done in bringing down that wall and staying engaged in the conversation. Where there's no engagement, there's little hope.

FOCUS ON FEELINGS

Another very typical hurdle to effectively resolving differences is our tendency to focus on a behaviour, rather than the emotional injury that behaviour causes. I think this is one of the most important aspects of conflict resolution. It would solve so many problems – and even prevent divorces – if more people were able to take it on board.

When people raise complaints or have arguments, what you'll typically hear are statements like, 'I wish you would check with me before you make plans for us', or 'You never make the effort to spend time with my family', or perhaps, 'My friend always ditches me as soon as she's got a new boyfriend'. Every time there is a complaint about a behaviour, there is also an emotional injury being expressed. If you never check with me before you make plans for us, I might be feeling disrespected. If my friend ditches me every time she gets a new boyfriend, I probably feel unappreciated and hurt.

When you focus on someone's behaviour, your grievance is usually shared with an air of annoyance

"Every time there is a complaint about a behaviour, there is also an emotional injury being expressed."

or frustration. As a result, the other person will often become defensive and find a way to justify themselves. But when you share your more vulnerable emotions, such as the need that hasn't been met or the injury caused, the other person is more likely to respond with empathy and connection – especially if they truly care about your feelings. The key is to be willing to be vulnerable and tell the truth about how you're feeling.

RUPTURE AND REPAIR

Any kind of conflict or disagreement creates a rupture in a relationship. A rupture is fine as long as there's quick action to repair it. During your early years when your relationship blueprints were being created, you would have had your first painful experience of someone you love being angry or upset with you. This is also where you learned important lessons about relationship repair. If you got into trouble, but you knew your mum or dad would still be there for you, you internalised the important lesson that just because someone's mad at you doesn't mean they don't love you – that is, conflict doesn't mean rejection.

This willingness to repair ruptures is one of the foundations of a secure attachment. If you haven't internalised that sense of emotional security, conflict can feel especially threatening. Perhaps you didn't have the best role models to show you how to manage relationship conflict. If you grew up in a household where there was anger or violence, you might be hyper-sensitive to even the subtlest hint that someone's not happy with you. This is often the case with people who have an anxious attachment style.

If you grew up in a home where nobody ever talked about what was going on and there was an environment of secrecy, you may be unskilled in expressing your emotions, so you tend to avoid difficult conversations altogether, perhaps resorting to making passive aggressive comments, sulking, walking out of the room mid-argument or even walking out of the relationship entirely. These are all signs of an avoidant attachment.

If too many ruptures occur without adequate repair, the foundations of trust and emotional connection can begin to crumble. It's incredibly important to find ways to disrupt those old, automatic patterns and create a new, healthy way to relate.

THE ART OF APOLOGY

An apology that's poorly executed can do more damage than no apology at all. If you've ever been on the receiving end of an insincere apology, you'll know it can feel insulting and insensitive. There are several versions of non-apology, and they often sound like: 'I'm sorry you feel that way', 'I'm sorry if I offended you', or 'I'm sorry, BUT ...'. A genuine apology takes full responsibility for your actions or words, acknowledges the hurt you've caused, and expresses genuine remorse. Even better, it should include a commitment to changing your behaviour.

Many of us as children were taught to just say sorry, whether we meant it or not, and whether we truly felt we were in the wrong or not. I suspect that may be why we default to an insincere apology, thinking a quick 'sorry' will smooth out relationship tension, or sometimes refuse to say sorry at all.

THE POWER OF POSITIVITY

One of the best predictors of how a conflict will turn out is the mood and emotional tone of the relationship before the argument begins. If you're both feeling pretty good about each other, you're more likely to weather the occasional storm, whereas if there is frequent negativity and limited warmth or affection, the emotional toll of an argument can be hard to overcome.

As a rule of thumb, relationships need five positive interactions for every negative one to keep things sailing along in a happy direction. A positive interaction can be as small as a touch on the arm, making eye contact, checking in with a cheery text message and being fully present during a conversation. These are the gestures and cues that signify enjoyment, commitment and delight in each other's company. When the ratio goes out of balance and there is more negativity, hostility or emotional distance, it becomes more difficult to recover from conflict.

HOW TO ARGUE WELL

Allow for different conflict styles

Understanding mismatched communication styles allows you to make compromises. For example, the volatile communicator might write a letter or send an email to vent their frustrations in a way that isn't as confronting and overwhelming. The avoider might set in place a time limit on arguments, and take frequent breaks to regulate their emotions.

Maintain the 5:1

Make it a priority to inject five positive interactions into your relationships for every negative one. These don't have to be grand gestures, but the more people know you appreciate and value them, the less damage that will be done by the occasional conflict.

Stay in the game

In any relationship, the biggest challenge to overcome when there is disagreement is when one person withdraws from the exchange. Walking out, refusing to talk or even brushing things off and pretending nothing is wrong will undermine any prospect of meaningful connection.

Step nine

LET GO OF PAST PAIN

Every relationship will involve minor infractions.

In our busy, preoccupied lives, it's easy to be unintentionally thoughtless. Someone might forget an important date or cancel plans, not realising how important the event was to you. Harsh words can be spoken in the heat of the moment. If the relationship is important enough, we normally choose to let go of these minor hurts. Holding on to small grievances creates uncomfortable and unnecessary rifts in otherwise positive relationships.

But then there are those wounds that run a lot deeper and leave more permanent scars. If your partner is unfaithful, a friend betrays your confidence or a parent was never there for you in the way you wanted them to be, the damage can be hard to undo, and you might not ever salvage the relationship. In those situations, there's a lot more healing to be done and tough decisions to be made, but ultimately it's still up to you to decide if you will allow that past, painful experience to influence your present and your future.

Pain from past trauma or abuse can have a significant impact on your physical and emotional wellbeing, and can make it difficult to fully trust people. Letting go and moving on when someone has hurt you is often easier said than done. If someone has mistreated, disrespected or betrayed you – or worse – it's no small thing to dissolve those painful emotions and move on, unencumbered by anger and resentment. You may ask yourself whether you would even want to. Wouldn't it be weak or foolish to let someone off the hook?

You might worry that if you let go of the pain that serves as a reminder of what you've suffered in the past, you'll open yourself to the possibility of experiencing the same thing again. We all have an instinct for self-preservation, which is why harmful experiences imprint on us so strongly and leave a lasting emotional residue. The idea of letting go and forgiving someone understandably brings up a lot of complicated thoughts and feelings.

IS IT NECESSARY TO FORGIVE?

In the past three decades, there has been significant research conducted into the benefits of practising forgiveness. One meta-analysis of 12 studies involving participants who had experienced a range of injustices, from marital conflict to sexual assault, concluded that people experienced significant improvements in mood following a structured forgiveness process. Most experienced reduced rates of depression, stress and distress, and a boost in positive emotions. So, there is some evidence that learning a process of forgiveness has good outcomes.

Clinical psychologist and author Dr Harriet Lerner is one of the most prominent voices in the area of anger and betrayal in relationships, having written a dozen books on the subject. Interestingly, based on her research and clinical experience, she doesn't believe it's necessary to forgive. She does, however, recommend you find a way to let go of past hurts so that they don't continue to taint your future relationships.

WHAT FORGIVENESS MEANS

People often struggle with the idea of forgiveness because of the meaning they give it, so perhaps the best place to start is with a shared definition. In psychology, we generally define forgiveness as a conscious choice to release feelings of anger or vengeance towards a person or group of people who've harmed you, regardless of whether they deserve it or not. Note that releasing feelings of vengeance is not the same as condoning unacceptable behaviour, and it has nothing to do with mending fences or resurrecting a broken relationship.

Let's be clear: you can forgive someone and still never have contact with that person again. And if you do have contact – perhaps because you share children or belong to the same family – it simply means you choose to drop the hot, angry emotions that are ultimately robbing you of your own inner peace, and no longer allow those old wounds to have any part of your present experience.

When you truly understand what forgiveness is, you realise it's not 'soft' or weak-willed. In fact, it's the ultimate act of courage and empowerment. Forgiveness means choosing to no longer allow another person and

> "Forgiveness means choosing to no longer allow another person and their behaviour to take up precious space in your mind or rob you of your joy, peace or self-worth."

their behaviour to take up precious space in your mind or rob you of your joy, peace or self-worth. What we also know for sure is that anger is toxic. The stress that it places on your body over the long term increases your risk of disease and even death. There's a Buddhist saying that holding on to anger or resentment is like picking up a hot coal to throw at another person. There's a lot of wisdom in that.

PRACTISING ACCEPTANCE

Fred Luskin is Director of the Stanford University Forgiveness Projects. After many years of research, and working with thousands of people, he has distilled the essence of forgiveness into one simple concept: to be willing to make peace with the word 'no'. For example, you may have wanted your partner to be faithful to you, and their answer, as demonstrated by their actions, was 'no'. You wanted your best friend to be more supportive of you during a time of need. You wish your father had been more present when you were growing up. You had an expectation that someone important to you would keep your confidence, and yet they betrayed you.

It's a simple but powerful way of focusing your attention on the precise cause of your suffering. Regardless of whether you had a right to expect something different or if you deserved better, the reality is that you didn't get what you wanted, needed or expected, and that hurts. Dr Luskin uses the term 'unenforceable rules' to describe the things we want but can't have. We have social rules and personal values that dictate the kind of behaviour we expect from people, but ultimately we have no way of forcing them to behave in the way we would like.

That's painful, but it's the hard truth. The more we recognise the role that unenforceable rules are playing in our relationship conflicts, the more peace we might feel. Simply put, we learn to let go of the things we can't control and focus our energy on what we can, such as our own daily habits and choices, our own values and integrity, and where we choose to focus our attention.

In mindfulness- and acceptance-based approaches to therapy, we place a heavy emphasis on the importance

> "We have social rules and personal values that dictate the kind of behaviour we expect from people, but ultimately we have no way of forcing them to behave in the way we would like."

of acceptance as a path to reducing emotional suffering. Acceptance in this context means having the willingness to meet your experience exactly as it is. For years I've told my clients, regardless of the particular problem they're grappling with, that the root cause of their suffering is the gap between how things are and how they'd like them to be. This is a universal experience. We convince ourselves that our happiness lies on the other side of that gap, and if we can't bridge the gap, it's the unwillingness to be at peace with the way things are that creates the mental struggle. Practising acceptance is twofold. There is the willingness to accept the outer circumstances of our lives, especially in situations where we have no control. And then there is the willingness to feel our own painful emotions.

FEEL YOUR FEELINGS

When someone has hurt you, it's appropriate to feel hurt, angry and sad. Acknowledging and feeling the pain is the first step on the path to healing. Before you have any hope of forgiving someone for the hurt they've caused you, there first need to be time and space to grieve. Attempting to move from pain to forgiveness without fully feeling the pain of that disappointment is like trying to leapfrog over the hard part. We humans are not great at sitting with discomfort, and we come up with all sorts of strategies to try to avoid, escape, minimise or suppress our feelings. But any attempt to fast-track forgiveness as a way of avoiding your raw emotions is unlikely to succeed.

Connecting with anger can be healthy, especially if you've learned to bury angry feelings. Anger can be a sure sign of a boundary violation, or an alert to an injustice that needs your attention. We don't want to demonise anger, but we also need to recognise that sometimes focusing on our anger is a protective cover for more vulnerable emotions, such as rejection, sadness or humiliation. Anger can also be really bad for you.

In the two hours following an angry outburst, people are twice as likely to experience a heart attack and are also at greater risk of having a stroke. Even thinking about incidents from the past that made you angry reduces your immunity.

When the incident has passed, we don't necessarily want to keep bringing it into our present, with all its damaging consequences to our physical and mental health. Ideally, you want to feel those feelings as a way of healing them and releasing them. Journalling can be a simple and highly effective tool for getting all your feelings out, and has been proven to reduce the long-term negative consequences of that pain.

"Acknowledging and feeling the pain is the first step on the path to healing."

DON'T STAY STUCK IN THE STORY

When you've been hurt, it's very tempting to rehash the painful details over and over again in your mind. You might even have friends you get together and co-ruminate with, which essentially means that you keep asking each other about the incident, bringing it up in conversation, raging about how awful it is and never putting it to rest. When you continue to revisit the painful experience, focusing on the injustice and the betrayal, you only perpetuate your suffering. When people say they have trouble moving on from painful feelings, it usually means that they have trouble unhooking from the story.

Mindfulness exercises can be a great way to learn to notice those thoughts trying to come in and to gently guide them back out again. You don't need to push them down or try to block them out (believe me, it doesn't work); you simply acknowledge the thought rising up and watch it pop, like a bubble rising to the top of a fizzy drink.

FIND THE GIFT

The people who are most likely to experience genuine forgiveness and even compassion for those who have hurt them are also the ones who typically go on to use their pain for the greater good. Rather than allowing pain to shrink them or harden them, they channel energy into a cause or project that helps others who might be experiencing something similar. Using your own pain in the service of a greater good can be a powerful way to heal.

STEPS TO LETTING GO

Sit with discomfort

When I say to be present to your pain, I mean sitting
in meditation and connecting with the emotions in
your body, or writing down what you feel in a journal.
Sitting with discomfort doesn't mean ruminating
or rehashing the details of an event in your mind.
It means allowing yourself to acknowledge the depth
of your emotions as a way of healing.

Practise compassion

When there has been pain, we can sometimes be our own worst enemies, making a bad situation worse with our own harsh and critical thoughts. Practise being kind to yourself and offering yourself the same tenderness that you would to a friend who had been through what you have.

Remember our shared humanity

In life there is suffering, and no-one escapes it. Even
the person who hurt you has their own challenges and
pain to deal with. When we connect to the universal
experience of human suffering, this helps us to feel
less alone in our own pain. Whatever you've gone
through, someone else has experienced it too. This
isn't intended to diminish your experience, but to
remind you you're not alone.

Step ten

BE GRATEFUL FOR EVERY EXPERIENCE

I remember a conversation I had with a good friend when I was in my early twenties. I'd been thinking of breaking up with my boyfriend and was feeling a bit conflicted about it.

I remember my friend saying to me, very matter-of-factly, that yes, it's hard, but at the end of the day, 90 per cent of relationships don't last, so why take it so much to heart? I was shocked. *Where did you get that statistic? That's devastating*, I thought. Truth be told, I think she made it up, but what she said next was illuminating. She asked me, 'How many boyfriends have you had so far?' Quick mental count ... hmmm ... maybe five. 'How many of them are you still with now?' Oh ... just the one. Now her made-up statistic made perfect sense. Most relationships aren't forever, and that's okay.

If you look back over your life and count all the classmates, roommates, workmates, close friends, family friends and friends of friends, hundreds of people have probably come and gone. If you're lucky, some of those relationships have deepened into a strong and lasting connection. Some might have ended abruptly and left a scar, while others just fizzled out due to a lack of time and attention.

Hopefully you now have a toolbox of resources that will help you to shore up those connections that you know you'd like to hold on to. However, when a relationship ends, it's often not intentional and there's no ill will between you. People fade out of your life, and if they reappear later, you happily reconnect.

If a friendship is casual and you decide there's not enough common ground to make you want to pursue it further, it's not unusual to let it dissolve with little fanfare. You might just become less available for a while, until eventually the invitations stop coming.

Often, whether a relationship lasts or not is more by chance than by design.

It's not very direct, but where there's limited emotional investment, it's usually not a big deal, and there's no real collateral damage.

But sometimes you need to make a choice to end an important relationship. And sometimes another person makes the choice to end a relationship with you. How do you navigate the complex emotional terrain of walking away from a partnership (whether romantic or platonic) with your head high and your heart whole?

HOW TO TELL SOMEONE IT'S OVER

It's a mistake to assume that when a relationship ends, it's harder for the person who has been rejected than the person who makes the decision to end it. Most of us are reluctant to hurt people we've cared about, even if it's clear you can no longer remain in a relationship with them. Obviously, there are going to be different considerations, and perhaps a different kind of emotional fallout, depending on whether you're ending a friendship or a romance, but if someone has played a significant role in your life, the fundamental principles are the same.

Be honest

People deserve to be told the truth, even if it's hard to hear. It's always best to have this conversation in person, but if you're worried about being overwhelmed by your own or the other person's emotions, you might write out all your thoughts and feelings in a letter. If a person has meant something to you, a text message doesn't convey the level of respect the relationship deserves.

Most of us will do anything to avoid confrontation, and this can be especially true if you have an avoidant or anxious attachment style. Avoidant people find it enormously uncomfortable to be with their own and other people's vulnerable emotions. They're much more likely to clam up completely or even 'ghost' someone (which is about the most cruel and confusing thing you can do to a person, so please don't do that).

If you're more anxious, you might become so consumed with worry about how the other person is going to react that you sidestep the issue, make excuses, send mixed signals and avoid being direct. In either case, your inability to manage your own emotions creates more confusion and hurt than if you'd just told the truth. Remember that you are responsible for your choices, your communication and maintaining your integrity. You can't be responsible for someone else's happiness, but you can do your best to be kind, and honesty is the kindest choice you can make.

Be decisive

Sometimes as a way of softening the blow, you might find yourself making all sorts of compromises that ultimately don't feel good for you and just send mixed messages to the other person. If you've ended a romantic relationship, it's usually not a great idea to try to be friends – at least not until you've spent enough time apart to be able to start again with a clean slate.

If you attempt to end a relationship and find yourself being drawn into lengthy negotiations, debates or guilt trips, it's important to hold your line. If someone is demanding that you explain for the hundredth time why you're making this decision, it's okay to withdraw from the conversation. Any compromise on your part can open the door to more demands, and you may soon find yourself back where you started, having the hard conversation all over again. It's better for both of you if you stand your ground.

Own your part

We've established pretty clearly that each person in a relationship has a responsibility to own their part in it. When choosing to walk away from any kind of partnership, it can be tempting to shine a spotlight on all of the other person's faults and flaws, because that makes it easier for you to justify your decision. This is self-protective – focusing on the other person's faults may relieve you of your own doubt and uncertainty. But it can also be a convenient way to deflect attention from your own shortcomings and whatever role you've played up until this point. I'm not suggesting you default to, 'It's not you, it's me!', because that will always sound like a cop-out. But I am suggesting that as part of being honest and acting with integrity, you don't absolve yourself of responsibility entirely.

DEALING WITH REJECTION

The pain of rejection lights up the same areas of the brain as physical pain. It really hurts. When someone you care about tells you they don't want you in their life anymore, either through their words or their actions, it's natural to experience grief, sadness, confusion and even anxiety. If they just stop returning your calls with no explanation whatsoever, that's painful and confusing. A close friend or romantic partner is more than just one person in your life. They represent a shared history, plans for the future, familiar and comfortable routines, mutual friends, and someone you've counted on for love and support.

Move towards acceptance

The only way to find peace in the face of any painful life event is to fully accept the reality of the situation. Acceptance is a process, especially if the ending has come as a shock to you, and you might struggle with intense resistance at first. Rejection activates your attachment system, and the most natural and instinctive response is to protest and make attempts to reconnect. You might feel waves of anger, regret, denial or confusion, or you might try to negotiate another chance to work things out. Ultimately, if there is to be any chance of a new, different relationship moving forward, it needs to start with acceptance of the situation as it is right now.

Feel your feelings

When we feel particularly vulnerable emotions like sadness, abandonment or humiliation, it can be tempting to cover them with anger, which feels more empowering, or to counterattack with defensiveness and blame. It's important to acknowledge what you really feel. When you give your emotions space to be fully felt, they tend to pass more quickly than if you suppress or deny them. The temptation to block your emotions with alcohol, food or other distractions can be strong, but ultimately those feelings will still be there waiting for you, so you might as well face them head-on.

Don't bring the past into the present

Being rejected can open old wounds from your past. If you have an anxious attachment style, you might obsess over the situation and drive yourself to a state of despair. If you're avoidant, your pattern will be to shut off your emotions completely. Old schemas may trigger feelings of abandonment, defectiveness or shame. If you can ask yourself, 'When have I felt this way before?' and recognise how much of your pain is attached to old wounds, it can be a powerful path to healing.

MOVING ON

Regardless of the nature of the relationship or whose decision it is to end it, there are some important steps you should both take to support your healing, growth and happiness, and to ensure you don't carry any emotional baggage into your future relationships.

Give it time

Depending on how long you've known someone or how long you've been in a relationship, it can take around three months before you really recover from a break-up. Trying to rush back to happiness can be a mistake. According to William Bridges, who wrote *Transitions: Making Sense of Life's Changes*, during any major life transition there is a period after the ending and before the new beginning which he calls 'The Neutral Zone'. This is the murky, confusing place where the old way of life has gone but you're not quite sure what the new way looks like yet. It can feel empty and dark, and is often a time for withdrawal and retreat, inner reflection and alignment with important values. This is the place where healing occurs, but the uncertainty can feel incredibly uncomfortable. This is why people are often desperate to either go back to the way things were or jump straight into something new. It's important to spend time in the neutral zone.

Limit contact

Most experts agree that in the early stages of a relationship ending, the best thing for both of you is to have no contact at all. It's so tempting to reach out and check in, to ask more questions or to feel you need 'closure', but more communication often just prolongs your suffering. Lean on your other friends and family for support to heal, but don't try to seek comfort from the person who hurt you.

Consolidate positive memories

It's fair to say that at some point in every relationship, there were happy moments. If you entered a relationship and chose to continue it for a period of time, even if things didn't ultimately turn out how you would have liked, for a time you were happy. There's no reason to cast the whole experience in a negative light or consider it a waste of your time just because it ran its course, or even if it ended badly. Remember the good times, even if it feels painful. Ultimately, this is much more healing than holding on to bitterness and resentment.

END THINGS WELL

Be grateful for every experience

How have you grown? What have you learned? What
memory will you cherish? What good might come
from this? When something crumbles, there are often
nuggets of wisdom buried in the rubble, if only you
choose to look for them. And in any situation, no
matter how painful, there is always something to be
grateful for.

Know your worth

The end of a relationship, whether it's your choice or not, can be a blow to your self-esteem. You may question your own judgement or your self-worth. Know that you are not defined by this or any other experience, but by how you choose to respond, the personal qualities you demonstrate and the values you uphold.

Look forward with positivity

Life and relationships are an adventure and an opportunity for joy, challenge and growth. Fill your heart with gratitude and look ahead with optimism and faith that the world is full of people ready and willing to love, support and value you for the exquisite creature that you are. You deserve only the best, and the best may be yet to come.

Acknowledgements

I'm grateful to everyone who has read and shared
their positive feedback on the first two *Crappy
to Happy* books, and who insisted I write the
third in the series. To everyone who has listened
to the *Crappy to Happy* podcast, left a positive
review, emailed or messaged me, I read all of your
comments and appreciate every one of them.

My husband, Mel, has, as always, been my
greatest cheerleader and supporter, getting up
with me in the early hours of the morning and
bringing me coffee when the manuscript deadline
was looming. Thanks to my parents for all their
love and support, and my daughter, Annabelle,
who dutifully checks the shelves in every
bookstore and moves my books to the front.

Thanks to the team at Hardie Grant who have
been endlessly patient and flexible with deadlines,
especially when a global pandemic upturned all
of our lives. In particular, thanks to Pam for the
opportunity to write another book so I can have
the boxset I've always wanted and Joanna for

all your help getting book three into the world. I'm very grateful to Vanessa at Red Dot Scribble, who has brought her editing expertise to all three of the *Crappy to Happy* books, tightening up the text, asking insightful questions and offering valuable suggestions.

I've learned so much from experts in the field of relationships and psychology whose work has helped me in my own life and in my client's lives. In particular, I've been inspired by the work of Dr Sue Johnson who developed emotionally focused therapy for couples, an approach to relationship counselling based on attachment theory, and Drs John and Julie Gottman for their decades of research into what makes relationships work.

I'm especially grateful to the friends who allowed me to share their stories in this book. Their names have been changed but they know who they are. I appreciate your willingness to share your experience for the benefit of others.

Published in 2021 by Hardie Grant Books,
an imprint of Hardie Grant Publishing

Hardie Grant Books (Melbourne)
Building 1, 658 Church Street
Richmond, Victoria 3121

Hardie Grant Books (London)
5th & 6th Floors
52–54 Southwark Street
London SE1 1UN

hardiegrantbooks.com

 A catalogue record for this
book is available from the
National Library of Australia

Crappy to Happy: Love Who You're With
ISBN 978 1 74379 679 5

10 9 8 7 6 5 4 3 2 1

Cover and text design by Alissa Dinallo
Typeset in Gotham Book by Kirby Jones

Colour reproduction by Splitting Image Colour Studio
Printed in China by Leo Paper Products LTD.

 The paper this book is printed on is from FSC®-
certified forests and other sources. FSC® promotes
environmentally responsible, socially beneficial and
economically viable management of the world's forests.